HOMECOMING

DIANNE EBERTT BEEAFF

HOMECOMING

HAWKMOON PUBLICATIONS
TUCSON, ARIZONA

HOMECOMING
Copyright © 1997 by Dianne Ebertt Beeaff

All rights reserved under Internatonal and
Pan American Copyright Conventions.
Published in the United States of America.
No part of this book may be used or
reproduced without written permission
except in the case of brief quotations.
For information or additional copies
address Hawkmoon Publications,
7502 E. Calle Cabo, Tucson, Arizona 85750.

Illustrations by Dianne Ebertt Beeaff

Cover: "Long Meg and Her Daughters
Stone Circle - Cumbria"

ISBN: 0-9656188-0-3
Library of Congress Catalog Card Number: 96-79342

For my mother and father
Edna and Russell Ebertt

and

For Dan, Danielle and Dustin for
sharing so many moments.

CONTENTS

Homecoming   1
Canterbury Cathedral   3
Battle Abbey in the Rain   5
Sea Hunger at Beachy Head   7
Storm Over Dartmoor   9
The Road to Chysauster   10
The Mermaid of Zennor   11
Aquae Sulis   13
Lustleigh Tea House   14
Athelhampton Hall   15
A Great Wind at Leeds Castle   16
Zennor by Night   18
The Bells of Tintagel   20
Mary Catherine, Lake Kate   21
Athelhampton Chantry   23
The Ullswater   26
Land's End   29
Passing Cadre Idris   30
Rain Over Hadrian's Wall   31
East Anglia's Fenlands   33
York   36
On Rannoch Moor   37
Through Kirkstone Pass in Cumbria   39
Duntuln Castle   40
The Shadow   42
The Pass of Glencoe   45
Glen Shiel   46
Lanyon Quoit   48
St. Mary's By the Springs -- Fountains Abbey   50
Clan Donald's Highlander   53
Elsdon Churchyard   54
Dunwich, Suffolk   56

Contents

Borley, Essex 57
Wayland's Smithy's Chambered Tomb 58
Willows Out of Oxford 59
The Isle of Skye 61
The Rollright Stones 62
London 63
Long Meg and her Daughters 65

ILLUSTRATIONS

The Vill of Christ Church Cathedral, Canterbury   2

Stone Row, Down Tor, Dartmoor. Reproduced with permission from Wildest Britain, Blandford Press, Poole, Dorset, 1986   8

The Queen's Bath, Leeds Castle, Kent   17

The Parish Church of St. Mary's, Puddletown, Dorset (Athelhampton Chantry)   24

Land's End, Cornwall   28

The Denver Windmill, East Anglian Fens   34

The Shadow. From a painting in the Marble Hall of the Cardiff, Wales City Hall. Painted in oils by E. Blair Leighton in 1909   43

Lanyon Quoit Prehistoric Burial Chamber, Cornwall   49

Window at Fountains Abbey, North Yorkshire   51

Sunset on the Isle of Skye   60

Long Meg and Her Daughters Stone Circle, Cumbria   64

PREFACE

I have had a life-long affinity with most things related to the British Isles. My first visit some years ago was "a sort of homecoming", to quote the poet Paul Celan. This collection was inspired by that trip. In my artwork I like to work in pencil because it is full of light. It allows for delicate shadow tones, subtle textures and a crisp delineation of shape through strong contrast.

Great Britain has a powerful and distinctive sense of place -- "old far-off things and battles long ago." But it's the little moments that make up life. Timeless continuities, the struggles and triumphs of life and living, these things transcend time and space and it is these universals which I have tried to capture in this book. Life presents us with all the possibilities of finding our way back home. This book represents one.

HOMECOMING

HOMECOMING

The land folds up for winter;
grasses brown and brittle;
sea winds thick and focused;
rock walls trailing off
into mist-grey
English stability
into permanence and charm.

There are other places. . .
elsewhere. . . no doubt.
Afloat on a dim sea,
lost in a shroud of sea fog,
the pale lamps we light
against the darkness
are many and varied.

Every journey
must have a soul.
Ours is the soul of
a place waiting
for someone
to come home.

The Vill of Christ Church Cathedral, Canterbury

CANTERBURY CATHEDRAL

Footstep through the Ville of Christ Church
In the ochre light of October past,
So nearly gone -- sunlight in the trees
And shadows on the face of Bell Harry --

To Canterbury, a sudden splendor of peace and power,
Of pinnacle and prism, this glitter
Of ecclesiastical might, wrought in stone
And space and light and line,

A testament to force of will; to artistry.
A profound holiness. "This is none
Other than the House of God. And
This the Gate of Heaven."

*   *   *

Walk on to Evensong, in the candled
Darkness of the quire, here lavished with care.
'Salvatormundi' sounding on the iron crash and echo
Of unseen wooden latches, rebounding,

Uplifted to heights of celestial silence.
A chasm of complaisance?
Distorted magnificence? A riddle.
So far from misery, the ennobled;

So far from desolation, the exalted;
So far from innocence, the corrupt.
On the swish and sweep of priestly vestments
Rides our separation. For the way's worn smooth

And shiny from here to there. But set aside
The motive and manipulation, the razzle-dazzle
Ritual for the ignorant, the fearful
And the powerless. Set aside the warriors

Mythologized in effigy, under a coat of arms.
One the same, who spoke -- who speak --
To those beneath with thunder and with threats;
Who lodge here their greatest and their good;

Who carve the stone and lay the crypt
And frame the brass plaque up against the long wall
Top to bottom. All souls saved with a sword
And a sovereign. The rest gone on to weed and willow

In the parish church.

So even, song. "Gloria in te domine".
The shift and shimmer fainting in candlelight
Through space and color. Go on then
To the Undercroft, a bay of Norman arches.

   *   *   *

They've shut us in with candle wax and incense
And dim and dusted air, with walls grey as a
Cloudburst. Here simplicity. Arched and darkened,
Pillared in the shadows.

Hear simplicity!
Speak the name of God in the still air.
"This is none other than the House of God.
And this the Gate of Heaven."

BATTLE ABBEY IN THE RAIN

Battle Abbey in the rain.

Cold voices in stone;
Soft breathing in trees;
The veiled distance of time,
the long whisper of night,
curled 'round me
like flowing water.

Outside,
A great bulk of crumbled grey wall,
Timeless, ancient, formidable,
Sunken in shadow.
Empty-eyed vacancy
aglow with the grey-white shapes
of elemental spirit things.

Inside,
A great space of seeded airy gloom,
Fierce, solitary, mystical;
A wild October wind,
Black-lace branches
beating the air, beating the earth,
beating the walls.

black with night.
Stone cold pillars
pressed up against the living gale.
Imprints and shades;
The clash of battle, the smell of blood
and the colors of men gone.

The chant of monks, the smell of incense
and the colors of men gone;
Stitched in the stones;
Seared in the soil.

Battle Abbey in the wind.
Battle Abbey,
And those dead of night
in the dead of night.

Battle Abbey in the rain.

SEA HUNGER AT BEACHY HEAD

I stand alone on Beachy Head in a handful of rain.
Chalky cliffs, white-faced and streaked with soils,
drop off into the living air.

Behind me, in a smatter of hedges in brambles and fern,
whale-backed hills rise and fall like waves --
slope and hollow, slope and hollow, slope and hollow. . .
and sheep.

And directly below -- essence of ocean. Cream and brown
and molten grey crystal, etched in silver spray
and a deep-sea light to the far horizon.

Sea there has always been. Sea there will always be.
Endless as the wind, with neither time nor words.
Only a hiss and a whisper; a swell and a long roll.

The heaving silence of eternity.

Stone Row, Down Tor, Dartmoor. Reproduced with permission from <u>Wildest Britain</u>, Blandford Press, Poole, Dorset, 1986

STORM OVER DARTMOOR

The soul drifts upward to the moor
Where brooding spirit trees stand
In a grey October mist
And the wind moves great sheets of rain
Along the ridges of Hound Tor.
Windswept stone circles rise up
From the heather and the moor grass
Out of spiky gorse and rusted bracken.

Here on wild winter nights
The tinners and the peat cutters
And the wise old women
Gathered by the cottage fires
And huddled up for the beat of the rain
And the howl of the wind; told aged tales
Of mires and bogs and magical voices
From mirror-black peat-water pools.

The Dewerstone, Classenwell Pool in a clammy shroud,
The Wisht Hunt in full cry over Two Bridges,
And the Way of the Dead to Lydford.

On granite-grey moorstone
Soul birds in spectral white circle the cairns
Wreathed below, trailed in damp green mosses and fern.
A wild storm-beauty -- enchanted, forbidding;
Legends in bleak black hills
Their ancient muddied traces
Cut deep into the howling silence
Where spirit forces clamor through places
Only the soul can know.

THE ROAD TO CHYSAUSTER

Snake-thin and damp runs the way to Chysauster,
that bulk of ancient Cornish stone and timelessness
set firm in the amber of isolation.

Chunks of cloud shadow the land -- high, round and raw.
In the air, the sweetness of wet grass
warmed in the sunlight, sea-gulls in slanting flight
up the wind and the sounds of field and farm
worn water-smooth under the tongue.

On the grassy hill there, stand darksome stone walls,
rough-edged and wind-blistered. Iron ages old.
And here below stand darksome stone walls,
rough-edged and wind-blistered. Ages old.
The farmer in high boots and coveralls
sends the herd of milk cows gate to gate
along the hedgy row. Number 307, with her name,
passes by, one leg stiff and lifeless.
And the farmer flings an arm over the flank of her
and sees her through as slow as it takes,
with kindness and reassurance.

Iron ages old, he did the same.
Compassion not lost
in a world gone mostly mad.

THE MERMAID OF ZENNOR

In the parish church of St. Senara
Hard by the Cornish sea,
Where the winds go wild
Through land beguiled
With stone-circled sorcery,

So she sat and she sang each Sabbath morn
In a gown of sea-deep blue;
Her manner most free
Like an unfettered sea
And her hair had a corn-silken hue.

He a chorister there, Matt Trewhella by name --
It was he she had come to see --
On a howling wind day
She came up from the bay
Full seaborne; she set him free.

Into the stream by the village green
And down the stream to the sea,
For Pendour's Cove
The two of them strove
Tossed to windward and lee.

Now in Mermaid's Cove on a warm summer's night
In that grey and intemperate sea,
Matt Trewhella's voice rings
And Morvoren she sings
Of their love through eternity.

In the parish church of St. Senara
Hard by the Cornish sea,
Where the winds go wild
Through land beguiled
With stone-circled sorcery,

By the cold grey stones of a three-lighted wall
Still stands the Mermaid's Chair;
In a carved panel band
Glass and comb in hand
She, the Mermaid of Zennor, so fair.

AQUAE SULIS

Ancient Cotswold town on a ridge of blue clay;
In a circle of limestone. The great curve
of the river pooled east to west.

Celtic shrine and Roman spa.
Out of the Saxon twilight,
The medieval monk.

Bath. . .
In a wash of Georgian splendor;
Palladian facades and long colonnaded terraces
Drenched in old gold and moonlight.

LUSTLEIGH TEA HOUSE

The fire's afoot, the lamp glows,
Burnished in the rain.
Hollyhocks and primrose,
Bracken-bound in tangled rows,
Strewn along the lane.

Reeded roofs and snowy stone;
Shadow-dampened pools;
Earthy moss and green bone
Break the highland overgrown
In misted fairy stools.

See within the hearth-light warms
The soul, our tea and scones.
And winter-emptied trees and storms,
These come and go, beclouded forms,
On bared and bone-wet stones.

ATHELHAMPTON HALL

There's a deep blue mist
On Athelhampton Hall.
Beyond the gate-house --
In a cold hush and a touch of wind --
That great grey bulk
Of weathered stone
Fades with a gracious peace
Into the soft coolness
Of evening air.
And the blackened boughs
Of yew trees
Spread their dark shapes
Out over the grass.

Many-windowed;
Old, grey and tired;
Walls black with lichen
And dead red leaves.
Spirits settled in stone --
The plowman and the warrior --
Near enough to touch;
All in a glimpse of old things
And a single lighted lamp.

A GREAT WIND AT LEEDS CASTLE

Over Leeds comes a clean blue wind,
firm with the power of winter;
a solid, thick wind that hammers
blackened yews and chestnut trees,
their landscapes handmade
in apple green and sage.

With splendid strength
this great winter wind
beats up against the old stone
tower of the Gloriette;
a long deep howl of wind
that sounds around the room
hollow as thunder;
that moves up and down
the chimney with a roar and a groan
and leaves candlelight
flickering on bare walls.

The Queen's Bath, Leeds Castle, Kent

ZENNOR BY NIGHT

On a wild and empty night,
we came to Zennor in Cornwall,
Coaly black
in a great whistle of wind;
Galey weather raging all about,
darkish, wild-eyed,
sated with slanting trees
And woven spells.

Into the tumult we stepped,
opened the gate in a rock wall
set slate-blue and coarse
in a bouldered Cornish hedge,
and passed through.

Then up ahead, ancient, square-jawed,
the farmhouse opened up
and a shaft of yellow light
fell out over the grass
twisted in the farm-yard --
a swirl of cauldon vapors.

The racy winds played down on us
from high brooding hills
and bristling rocks;
Stirred imaginings
of the long, long dead,
dark powers and souls unseen;

Midnight sisters
huddled with winds to sell,
their knotted threads
dancing in a blur of winking light.
Charms and charmers;
Stone circles and sacred wells;
Cunning-men and conjurers.

Through the salt-laden sea winds,
raven-haired he came --
seven-league boots and a wishing cap --
black eyes burning dark-power secrets;
On through the wind and the rain
in the footsteps of a long past people.

"No rooms," he said. Regrets.
"Too late in the season," he said.
And turning on a blast of wind
and wizardry,
he left us alone again in the maelstrom.

THE BELLS OF TINTAGEL

The Bells of Tintagel
Sing down the wind.
Their glory unbounded,
Their voices resound,
Each listener uncrowned,
without and within.

The Bells of Tintagel
Shout from the heights.
St. Madryn implore.
They gladden. They soar.
Joyous encore
of the Spirit. Delights.

The Bells of Tintagel
Push out to sea.
Fishermen mark them.
Saint! Sinner! Hark them!
Life's dazzle's darkened
the Soul's rhapsody.

The Bells of Tintagel
Misted in time.
Ethereal, unearthly,
They call to us worthily,
Humanity's harmony,
the collective Divine.

The Bells of Tintagel
The Bells of Tintagel
The Bells of Tintagel
Go singing down the wind.

MARY CATHERINE, LADY KATE

Mary Catherine, "Lady Kate",
Here in-earthed, time gone by,
In shrouds of blackened loam
And dewy violet leaves;
Untroubled now -- as once she was --
In soundless sleep.

Iron fence, ruined and rusted,
Brindled stone on sunken hollows;
Time-worn, embellished in chiseled roses
And climbing vines
And the empty stone vases
That once were filled.

At hand on every side,
Course and stippled
Lichen-littered head-stones and vaults
Angled in the haze and hillside,
Incline to winter chill
And the breath of cedar smoke
Up from the valley.

This -- the season of dark nights.
Seven great and gloaming pines
Gone wild in a leaden sky.
This -- dark weather. Skyless.
Wispy at the edges.

Memorials, untenanted in soul,
Gather dusk to wrap
The stone, the bone, the cold black earth.
Over-clouded monuments these.
They slip away in sprays of moss and greenery
Along the footpath to the parish church.

So too, our own mortality,
Fated folly -- so finished.
Cloaked spirits and after-images,
Folded in a ring of giants.
Life -- once begun -- dissolved,
Illusory, ungrounded.
And we pause for Vespers,
Dirge and knell go silent
To drenched and dripping limbs,
Falling on the faces of the lamps
To lie alone.

She's taken the veil.
She lies entombed.
So shall we all.

Til then and after,
"God keep you, friend."

ATHELHAMPTON CHANTRY

Stillness, consumed in dust,
Shake us with visions gone;
With faded shadows and hallowed hands.
But leave behind the arms of war.

This Lady and her knight, Sir Martyn,
(Argent two bars gules),
In silk and satin
With daggers crossed
And folded hands,
Their seasons of honor,
Their luminous times have
Run a course to resignation.

The tunic, the broadsword, the shield;
The veil, the mantle, the robe,
Notched and pitted,
In Purbeck marble, in Ham Hill stone,
In moldered alabaster.
Saints and sinners
Chronicled in icy stone,
Cloistered in glacial chill
And pearly polish.

The Parish Church of St. Mary's, Puddletown, Dorset
(Athelhampton Chantry)

They've gone from the far green hill
Now misted in early winter rain;
Passed on into the rime and gloss
Of distance. Impermeable and winter-aged.

Stillness, consumed in dust,
Bring us like peace.
A wordless, breathless peace;
A fire in a glaze of frost.

THE ULLSWATER

Ancient enchantment -- the Ullswater.
A whisper of waves to the coming night.

There's a rustling in the thickets
And bushes bend with the wind.
Something more than solitude is here;
Something wind-blue and magical,
Something spread out among the trees
Like the long roll of the sea.
There should be phantom horns,
Long and low, through the pearl-pale mist.

Things happen here, they say,
Secret things
That move in the drift of time.
Hidden things
That lie in the hollow of the hills,
In the great dark wood,
In the line and ripple of the water
Now blotted with sunshine
And a low smolder of cloud.

The firm face of the mere shivers but once
And is stilled; a silver stone
Set in a cold light
With winter in the air. . .
And some One watching.

A sudden sharp shower of rain
Soaks the soul with solitude
And then again comes
That pale green glow that is evening;
And the great lake fades
Into the peace of night
With a shattering indifference.

Land's End, Cornwall

LAND'S END

Granite and white waves.

Land's End. . .
earthy isolation. . .
wild. . . windswept. . .
enveloped in secrets,
like a night fog.

The eternal sea
pounding
with steamy spray
in rolling rounds
like thunder.

Slanted gorse. . .
bent bramble bush. . .
scratching a living
in bare brown cliffs. . .
like love.

Granite and white waves.
Granite and white waves.

Forever.

PASSING CADRE IDRIS

Cadre Idris! Phantasm!
Into the half-light
we pause, spell-bound.

Shrouded black hulk
glinting silver.
Glassy ribbons
of light and water
shimmer mercurial,
one on one,
as in a dream.

Cadre Idris! Unbounded.
Above and below.
Shoulders in the mist;
Foot in a dark field.

RAIN OVER HADRIAN'S WALL

Dark sky, dark ground -- Housesteads in November.
A ghostly spot, strange and lonely,
Wrapped in the wet and cold of drifted centuries
And a scream of wind.

Out from the wilderness of hills and heather,
On to a shallow reedy bank
In the gloom of mist, cuts Knag Burn --
Down below the Wall.

The same skies fell for ancient Rome --
The African, the Spaniard. . .
In village shops and Pagan temples,
On rubbled ramparts running sea to sea.

And still the rain drops,
Round and thin,
Through the grand cold solitude
Of the North.

Darkness deepens daylight.
The sky has gone thin
And chill over
The soggy fields,

And the rain beats
In great blown
Sheets up against
The face.

Baretime...
Wide whirling winds.
Old things.
Endless hills.

Time eternal,
Measured Time,
Soaked together in

Rain.

EAST ANGLIA'S FENLANDS

The Fenlands, in this season of mist,
Roll out their flat black soils
Under low and slated clouds.
A sky-laden landscape of old sea-beds
Where vaporous patches of pearl glow --
The breath of the new dawn --
Wrap banks and dikes and meadows
In muted water-color washes.

Lapwings veer and reel against
Grey-stone towers. And seagulls
Mob the plow. And now and again,
When the sky splinters overhead,
Windswept hazes of twiggy oak
And ash and elm and poplar
Go marbled and midnight green
For a winter-whitened sun.

But the sky drops down again
To touch my cheek with
A pale spray of rain
And these send mild rivers
And man-made meres, willow-winged,
In a flux of silver, to the North Sea;
To marshes and mudflats wild with geese,
The horizon a level line of sea and sky.

The Denver Windmill, East Anglian Fens

In the vast flats of such rich
And inky earth, sit snug villages,
Saxon and Danish by birth,
With sagging pink weavers' cottages,
And over by the waterways,
Long and straight and muddied tracks
With meadows and pastures, lawn green
And coal black from Lincoln to Ely.

Once, though, this was a more watery world
Of barge-builders and turf-cutters
And wool merchants who broke the marshes
In places of glacial clays for the
Monks of Ely; where stilt-walkers --
Fowlers and fishers -- crept up and down
The meres and drainage ditches in punts,
For geese and duck and plover.

The Fenlands -- in darkness and in light.
In earth and air.
With winter hoar-frost on the reeds,
With windmills set against
The North Sea gales.
Yet here's a flat-bed truck,
A thunderous touch of rust-red
On the dusky underearth.

YORK

"York is too good to be true."

*   *   *

All of England lies here still,
in foot-worn stone,
the river and the distant hills --
fierce Brigantes rally against
Rome;
Eboracum, fortress on the Ouse and
Foss;
Eoforwic of the Angles, in ancient
Deira;
Viking Jorvik -- for 'the men of
the harbors'.

York -- second city of the realm;
a miracle in stone.
Guild-hall and gable and gateway
dappled in the red sun of winter;
a huddle of rooftops, towers and
spires.
And holy earth -- the Minster --
in silver-white lamplight,
horse-chestnuts scarlet from the
frost
and oak trees in buff and brown.

*   *   *

"York is too good to be true."

ON RANNOCH MOOR

The bogs of Rannoch Moor,
Bedeviled and drowned,
The Mountain and the Flood.
Fractured black pillars
In a seethe of yellow brome
And bare whistling heather.
Over-wet.
Over-black.
Above, no sky at all.

Across the upheaved water
The wind walks
On water-logged legs
And the rain follows,
A phantom, howling in shrouds
Over the witchy heath,
Haggard,
Water-pocked,
Lumps of fire-blackened stone.

Should we be lost
There'd be other murky specters
Dripping in forever twilight gloom
Cupped by the chilling fog.

Slipped under the low and the grey,
A no-color void clamps down
Over the dark earth.
Nothing above
But distant misted mountains
Spilling water ox-blood blue.
Nothing below
But wrecks of boiled stone,
Soggy lodgings
For moorish wiccan hags.

And over all, face down
In a smother of fear and trembling
Only blackness and the falling rain.

THROUGH KIRKSTONE PASS IN CUMBRIA

Ice-bound in the deep valley;
Brother's Water, Westmoreland --
blue as a king-fisher's wing
under the sun;

pale pebbly river
twisted in yellow brome
under a thread of cloud.

Then again:
Kirkstone Pass, a stony place
of black-rock scree slopes
sharp with the fear of expectation.

(Rowan shield and silvery sword,
black raven's wing and brindled hounds
and a dry-grass glow
like ashes, under a paley moon;
solitude and reed-fringed tarn,
beck water cold as crystal,
misted bracken banks
and witchy goldenrod
and crag-bound spirits
in a wail of rain.)

Ice-bound in the deep valley:
Brother's Water,
blue as a king-fisher's wing
under the sun.

DUNTULN CASTLE

The wind's come up on Duntuln
As banks of hail and wind --
A sluggish squall --
Gain the shore beyond.
Though here, the air stays blue
And swollen, grey-backed clouds
Scutter by on field and fence.
Silver-blue, the seas crest
And breach
The off-shore crags.
And yellow-brown, the highland
Grasses go flat under the great gale.

The wind's come up on Duntuln
And all about go things
That twist and turn
And bend and bear.
No rootless things, these. They persist.
A haven in rock-brown walls,
A sort of grounded circling
Where fragments stand apart,
Rough-edged,
With windows to the sea
And shades of ancient things
That bury time in weathered stone.

The wind's come up on Duntuln
Such winds uphold
The very weight of living;
Make mockery of power;
Take desolation and make solitude,
Take ruination and make strength,
Take isolation and make magic.
Such winds gather and set free
A timelessness
That defies both heart and mind,
Yet seizes the human soul
And presses on.

THE SHADOW

She stood beside him by the rampart wall,
His shadow there to fall
Against the cold and barren stone
When the sky unfurled; she'd be alone,
For he's to the wars
And she's for the waiting.

She could but pray he'd come again to her,
Like sunlight through a corner
Of the woods brings fire.
So bring him home; the same, no unfamiliar.
But he's to the wars
And she's for the waiting.

Raven's wing charred wood she took in hand
And traced his features and
Stood fair against the battlement.
For memory bright she marked him; with discontent.
For he's to the wars
And she's for the waiting.

Through hollows misted in the fields below
Return they must and so
Day and day she looked to find his face
But found him not; and death brought him to grace.
For he'd to the wars
And she'd to the waiting.

43

The Shadow. From a painting in the Marble Hall of the Cardiff, Wales City Hall. Painted in oils by E. Blair Leighton in 1909

For all who've gone, for all who've stayed,
To war -- from war -- dismayed,
With shadows thrown up against the wall --
Stand firm, be moved, protest; and break the fall.
No more to wars
No more for waiting.

THE PASS OF GLENCOE

Glencoe has a face full of tears,
A heart-load of sorrow.
In high rounded hills of whirling snow
And a sea of darkness,

Glencoe weathers her years
Like a widow
Under black veils of mist
And a wail of wind.

Glencoe, in mourning, disappears
In a shroud of shrieking rain,
Black body sliced with silver
As were those former lives of

Glencoe who, in bony mountain-fears,
Were lost when Campbell troops
From Argyll laid MacDonald
On the killing floor.

GLEN SHIEL

End of the world emptiness; spellbound;
The earth's long contours
Aflame with highland grass;
Silver streams gathered out of the moors,
And the shadowy burn below bound up
In mountain ash, willow and birch.

Cailleach, daughter of the winter sun --
All-Hallows to Beltane --
That terrible blue-faced hag
Has stepped out from the shieling hut
And called down the snow.
And Coaineag, the Weeper, incorporeal,
Wails in the darkness by a fall
Of white foam and steely grey.

Out of the bog grasses and the water weeds,
Out of the churn and tumble
Of the mountain's streams,
Shapeshifters and spirit masters --
The host of the Other World --
Move about in the air
In great clouds,
Up and down the face of the earth.

Over the burly bulk of Highland hills
Frayed with glistening rock and fallen water,
Over these bleak and burnt slopes,
In a float of mist,
The high and frosty heavens mirror the glow
Of last light and red-orange grass.

Polar strength and purity;
The terrible glory of the Highlands.

LANYON QUOIT

In the chill of a winter drizzle,
On an endless wind and a film of damp fog,
We come to Lanyon Quoit -- three uprights
And a capstone lost in their own dense shade
By the hollow road from Penzance.

In the poor lands of the West
Where the soils are acid and shallow,
There are no Stonehenge tombs
Of monumental splendor.
Only these, these ancient time-worn cromlechs
Despoiled by tin miners and moss,
Crook'd on the fierce Cornish uplands;
Only these, steeled provision for the dead
Of a dim past, spun out of verse
And chant and midsummer fire.

On the bleak winter ridge
The hills of the rise of day grow dark.
So too the stone cairn,
Those long gone within
Freed from stain and shadow,
Their sons gone down the ages.

And alone we stand, together now,
In the peace of eternal fields
And the open sky.

Lanyon Quoit Prehistoric Burial Chamber, Cornwall

ST. MARY'S BY THE SPRINGS -- FOUNTAINS ABBEY

And the great sun stood in a pearl-pale sky;
St. Mary's in a lace of leaves.
It's the season of peace that gives truth to the lie.
It's the light of our soul that she weaves.

The broad brimming brook in the still evening air
On the dust of our lives is cast;
For the beauty of time has colored her care
And her distance has colored her past.

Sancta Maria de Fontibus then,
And fair as a summer's rose,
Lonely the Skell, plain and humble her men,
Sound and sweet airs they gave her to know.

Great and greater she grew, thirty miles she snatched
To the west and whole villages vanished.
Prince and king, knight and bishop, her wealth more than matched;
Lives plowed under and villagers banished.

In the cause of her name, for her power and glory
Came rivals in sandal and stole.
Burned her wood to the ground without conscience or mercy,
Yet she rose greater still for the toll.

Then King Henry declared her dissolved and with others
She sank into death and decay.
Old, grey and weary, bereaved of her brothers,
She soundlessly faded away.

* * *

Window at Fountains Abbey, North Yorkshire

In the silence of night now, arc, bay and pillar
Under the witching moon,
Rise up -- showers of silver, woven in willow
Monastic, stone-vaulted, rough-hewn.

In her moonlit cloisters, in the sweep of her nave,
In the glinting of amber-hued lights;
In the rush of the river, so brooding, so brave --
A ribbon of living moonlight.

This is all that now stands of the power and the glory
That once brought great nobles despair.
But she's better for this -- for the end of a story
Begins when the heart is laid bare.

CLAN DONALD'S HIGHLANDER

In the frosty hours of the Western Isles' wide, unpeopled sky,
In a wall of wind and a pebbled rain set firm in soul and eye,

Shadow-chilled in ancient crags that rise to left and right,
Stone-hedged lanes grows small and small in the ashes of the night.

Alone he strides in a roll of mist, Dunvegan just below,
In kilt and plaid -- Clan Donald's dress -- the Highland hero-foe.

Broad blue bonnet, dirk and badge and silver buckled shoe,
Eye-bright and fair as day, yet no damp his tartan knew.

A kind of panic, small and sharp, came shrouded through the dark,
For when we turned to see him pass no soldier did we mark.

It has been said for long years past that the kilted men of Skye
In nightly whisperings, battle-clad, do come and go nearby.

MacDonald met MacLeod here, when the gorse was a sheet of flame,
Near Harta Corrie crags -- they say -- and oft now do the same.

Along the coast in the jagged rocks their shadows move like smoke.
The wraiths of men passed on before, three hundred years evoke.

So on we sped in that wild night to the harbor of Portree
Where lobster traps by ragged moon our daunted eyes did see.

Then steely footfalls echoed in the street of Stormyhill
And round about he came again, MacDonald, striding still,

Down past the white of Achmore House with grim finality.
Then all was still as death, once more -- the night, the rain, the sea.

ELSDON CHURCHYARD

A twist of winter wind, November blue,
Fresh from the Redesdale Moors,
Comes to Elsdon,
Stone-built in the Cheviot Hills.

And there on the Green --
So soon a place of clans and cattle --
There stands St. Cuthbert's
Low and grey,
The stillness of sacred stone
Toned by time and weather;
Full of her former days
And circled in green earth
And the wind among the trees.

In olden times, when Elsdon stood
On the drovers' track from Scotland,
There were reivers here,
And cattle lifters,
Stealing up and down the country.
Wild border folk
Given to riot and thieving.
In a blast of wind and rain they rode --
The lawless and the poor --
Up out of the Middle March
And across the sea-greens of the countryside.

At Chevy Chase, by Otterburn -- close by --
Douglas and Percy by moon-light
Struck each other down sword for sword,
The fallen English borne on 'biers of birch
And hazel grey' to Elsdon, in the Dean of Ellers,
Where the same long wind sweeps down
From high sandstone fells
To finger the shallow warrior graves
On Cuthbert's northmost side.
Memory deep,
Thought-burning like the sun.

St. Cuthbert's, brooding;
Elm trees black as winter
Dropping old leaves on the dead;
The rain in a great gust through the mist;
Black birds whistling
And cold drops on the eyes.

Sit a time in her wide cool shadows
Where bowmen grooved the pillars.
Then pass beyond to the peace of green things.
Here the soul stands alone when the sun is gone.

DUNWICH, SUFFOLK

Down to the sea at Dunwich,
Domnoc, "the deep place",
has gone under,
and the ghosts
of her long bells
lie smothered
in gold and brown.

Happy in the sun
her beach-bred fishermen
wade about in the shingled tide.

But give us a night
in a galey wind
and her muted church bells
shout from the seat
of time and the tempest
and leave us
silver from the sea.

BORLEY, ESSEX

Late autumn...
On an evening of black frost
And bright chill
We come to Borley in Essex,
On a hunt for phantom footsteps;
For the smell of incense
And violets out of season;
For bands of mist
And pale sad-eyed nuns
In inky robes.

At the very least...
Some dark and ancient village,
A winding country lane,
Overshadowed isolation,
Broken weedy walls.

But instead...
We come to Borley in Essex,
An open little hamlet --
Scattered cottages,
Sculpted bushes,
Tidied churchyard.
Prosperous...
Well-ordered.
And we slip away again...
Somehow deprived.

WAYLAND'S SMITHY'S CHAMBERED TOMB

On the dead true line of the Ridgeway Path --
that ancient track of the high downs --
lies Wayland's Smithy's Chambered Tomb,
a high place of death;
a clump of amazing greenness
and wet-black stones, in a mushroom mist,
a ring of iron-barked winter trees
and a spiral of ravens
flat and black into the sky.

Here too, in the dead rain of winter,
an unexpected gift -- poppies;
a few flutters of scarlet silk
singing in thin grey mud and a raw mist.

Earth-talk for 'life'.

WILLOWS OUT OF OXFORD

On a pale afternoon out of Oxford
Came a string of silver willows.
Full and fixed they were,
A great sweep of line and limb,
Bottom branches bared,
Tops like crystal fires --
The flash and glimmer of fused lights.

On a runaway sky,
With blue-ash clouds softly frayed
Against their backs, they stood --
This line of silver willows --
While up from thorn hedge
And mild midland rivers,
Came a stark October wind.

Why note at all
A string of silver willows
Fixed and full
Out of Oxford,
We of the million-footed
City, we of domes
And spires
And temples?

For we have all one breath,
And, with sublime indifference,
These willows
Catch the flash and play of life.
They stand,
The magic ointment
With which we may see fairies.

Sunset on the Isle of Skye

THE ISLE OF SKYE

On the high road from Staffin,
in that ancient place of Skye --
we are real.

    *   *   *

The flood of last light
gathers over the hills
and thickens the sky.
And from over Beinn Edro,
a hailstorm in black and white
races out to sea.

The darkness deepens
Great flakes of snow
drop out of the night.
Black firs, still
and cold on the far hills,
flatten and dissolve

in a vast bundle of mist.
Black towered mountains
washed with rain
and the great sea below
a broad metallic glitter.

Black mountains; silver sea;
Fragments of night
in a mesh of light.

THE ROLLRIGHT STONES

Down the tunnel of lane,
with bare branches,
bent to the breeze,
sounding on the air
like the rigging of a ship,

we reach the Rollright Stones,
squat, austere and greying
under a vaulted sky;
as gnarled and misshapen
as life itself.

A movement with no measure;
A song without sound;
A collective once removed.
Yet if we walked the inner path
We'd find peace.

LONDON

The spirit of London
glows in the dark. . .
enters the soul
from wet and shiny streets.

A vast forest of life,
the hum and roar
of the great city and
the spell of the silver Thames
move through the heart
like a dance.

"To be tired of London
is to be tired of life."

Long Meg and Her Daughters Stone Circle, Cumbria

LONG MEG AND HER DAUGHTERS

Long Meg lays a cold finger on the heart.
Earth magic in a howl of wind,
she leans for her daughters -- old ones all;
A great stone ring in thinning space
and bare twisted trees,
rain-water clear as light
soaks the sides of the living rock
and spirit things move unseen
through the wind.

Step in out of the rain.

The sky's in grey and black
and silver; the circled stones
a divine and perfect shape
of mist and magic;
Stand spell-bound
in that word-spinning
Celtic twilight
when stories were as good
as their words
and the circle held.

Step out of fear
and pain and sadness;
step out from the mire of the world
into the long light of hope --
with fire in your hand.

The circle holds;
Step out into the rain.

DIANNE EBERTT BEEAFF was born in Kitchener, Ontario, Canada. In 1968 she moved to Arizona and has lived in Tucson for twenty-one years working as a free-lance writer of periodical non-fiction. As an artist, she works primarily in graphite and watercolor and her work has been shown in a variety of local and national galleries. She is a member of the Southwest League of Fine Art and the National Federation of Press Women.

Additional copies of this book are available from:

HAWKMOON PUBLICATIONS
7502 E. Calle Cabo
Tucson, Arizona 85750